Ms. Grumble and Her Nonsense Words

A Book of Idioms

Tequilla Toy

Illustrations by Tamber Storment

ISBN
978-1-5437-5141-3 (sc)
978-1-5437-5142-0 (hc)
978-1-5437-5143-7 (e)

Print information available on the last page.

To order additional copies of this book, contact
Toll Free 800 101 2657 (Singapore)
Toll Free 1 800 81 7340 (Malaysia)
www.partridgepublishing.com/singapore
orders.singapore@partridgepublishing.com

05/28/2019

PARTRIDGE

Dedication:

This book is dedicated to children around the world. Remember, not trying is never an option.

Our teacher Ms. Grumble was at it again, saying things we didn't understand.

"Let's get ready for Math class. What's
8 x 8?"

"You can do it", said Ms. Grumble. "It's a piece of cake!"

Then up went the hand of Billy Sears.

"Thank you Billy," said Ms. Grumble.

"Now what's the answer. I'm all ears."

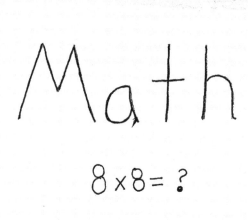

Math

$8 \times 8 = ?$

Ms. Grumble took us out for recess to play. Johnny Long had been picking on kids all day.

He shoved, he pushed oh he was tickled.
Ms. Grumble warned him to stop, or he'd
be in a pickle.

Lunch was no different. Ms. Grumble carried on with her words, saying some of the silliest things we'd ever heard.

The kids were noisy and throwing meatballs.

"Settle down boys and girls!" said Ms. Grumble.

"You're driving me up a wall!"

School was nearly at an end when Ms. Grumble gave out our homework and was at it again!

"Class go home and study the city of
Laredo. Don't go home and be a couch
potato!"

We looked at each other and began to ponder.

"What's a couch potato?" asked Sally Sumpter?

"Oh my!" said Ms. Grumble. "Seems my
words are a bit hazy. A couch potato
simply means don't be lazy."

Lazy! Now why didn't Ms. Grumble just say that?

Instead of all her nonsense words blah, blah blah!

Before we could leave we had to tell Ms. Grumble what we had learned.

I raised my hand and said, "We should all be bookworms."

Learn Your Idioms

Idiom	Meaning
a piece of cake	it's easy
I'm all ears	ready to listen
in a pickle	in a difficult position
driving up a wall	irritating or annoying
couch potato	lazy / lying on a couch watching television
bookworm	a person who spends a lot of time reading books

CPSIA information can be obtained
at www.ICGtesting.com
Printed in the USA
BVHW091339110619
550700BV00024B/1348/P

9 781543 751413